See!

by Cameron Grieft
illustrated by Anni Matsick

Core Decodable 1

McGraw Hill Education

Bothell, WA • Chicago, IL • Columbus, OH • New York, NY

MHEonline.com

Send all inquiries to:
McGraw-Hill Education
8787 Orion Place
Columbus, OH 43240

ISBN: 978-0-02-138925-4
MHID: 0-02-138925-X

Printed in Canada.

9 10 11 12 KOD 24

See the .

pencils

See the  .

paper

See the .

crayons

See the 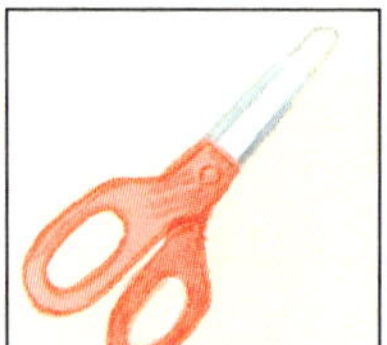.

scissors

See the  .

paste

See the  !

money